Save, Share, Simplify

How to Use the Sharing Economy to Reduce Expenses, Build Community, & Design Your Ideal Life

By Saul Of-Hearts

Published by Saul of Hearts
http://www.saulofhearts.com
First published in 2014
Copyright © Saul of Hearts, 2014
All rights reserved.

Cover photo by Saul of Hearts
Cover Design by Saul of Hearts

Publisher info:
Email: saulofhearts@gmail.com
Twitter: @saulofhearts

Contents

Introduction

In 2008, I graduated from film school in Boston and moved out to LA for the first time. As an East Coast native, it was a bit of a culture shock for me. I had to get used to driving everywhere and "networking" with other college grads to find work.

Not only that, but the timing couldn't have been worse. I arrived in LA just at the beginning of the economic crash. The film industry was reeling from a writer's strike, and my friends and I ended up in a series of dead-end jobs and internships.

Like many millennials, we quickly realized that **the old system wasn't working**. Here I was, just out of college, with student loans and car loans to pay, and the prospect of a "career", a family, and a house of my own was further off than ever.

Some of us turned to freelancing, whether or not we wanted to — there just weren't enough full-time jobs to go around. Others went to grad school or moved back home.

But as time went by, and several new economic trends started to emerge, I began to realize that maybe this transition wasn't such a bad thing after all. It was a curveball, sure, but it was also helping us realize **what was really important to us.**

Many of my peers were down-sizing, getting rid off all their extra stuff, so that even if they didn't earn a lot of money, they could still afford to travel or raise a family.

Others were forming **intentional communities**, large houses or shared by multiple residents who take turns cooking and cleaning, teaching each other skills, and helping out with gardening and art projects.

Even more were turning to the **Sharing Economy**: rather than accumulating things they didn't need, they chose to borrow, trade, rent, or share with their neighbors — everything from cars and spare bedrooms, to bikes, tools, and camera equipment.

I wrote this book with two audiences in mind. First, recent college grads and other millennials who feel like they don't fit in to the traditional employment system. If you're struggling to land a job or make a living, or just feel unfulfilled with your current life situation, this book will provide you an overview of some of the alternatives available to you.

Second, this book is for the parents and grandparents of millennials, who aren't really sure what their kids are up to these days. If you've ever thought to yourself, "Why is my grandson in a new country every time he calls home?" Or, "My daughter lets strangers sleep in her guest room — I'm worried about her!" Or even, "How can I get in on this blogging thing?" then this is the book for you.

One of the things I've noticed in my work is that many

millennials and their grandparents are at a similar crossroads in their lives. Since they aren't tied down by a full-time job or a family to support, both generations have **the freedom to try new things.** Many of the bloggers I meet are well in their 60s, and there are dozens of retired or semi-retired Taskrabbits who use freelance gigs as a way to supplement their income.

In the next twelve chapters, I'll introduce you to dozens of websites and organizations that can help you **save money,** meet people in your community, and live **the kind of life you've always wanted** — whatever that may be.

Since I've used most of these websites personally over the past few years, I'll share some **inside tips** as well as the **pros and cons** of each of these services. While your mileage may vary (literally), I've made thousands of dollars renting out my car, working freelance gigs, and using other online resources. I've also connected with hundreds of like-minded people all over the U.S.

I'm going to try and keep the technical talk to a minimum, although it helps if you have a basic understanding of smartphones and online services. Also, you'll need a Facebook or Paypal account to use some of these websites.

Here are just a few of the things you'll learn in this book:

— How to find affordable lodging while traveling, and connect with local tour guides

— How to safely rent out your car (and keep track of it the

entire time!)

— How to create a meal plan or trade skills with your neighbors

— How to find and book freelance gigs on your smartphone

— How to use online services to keep track of your finances and save money

This book is intended to be a broad overview of the Sharing Economy, not a comprehensive guide. My goal is to get you interested in these topics, and give you some ideas on how you can get started. So don't try to read it in one sitting — it's pretty jam-packed with information.

To get the most out of it, read it slowly and look up individual sites and services as you go. If you want to know more about a specific topic, check out the list of resources at the end of each chapter.

I can't make any guarantees that these ideas will work for you, nor is this book intended as financial, legal, or personal advice. The opinions in this book are my own. While I've earned money through some of these sites as a user of their services, I haven't been paid by any of these companies to recommend them.

Websites like these are changing all the time, so please be aware that some links and policies may have been updated since publication. If you have any questions or comments, let me know!

What is the Sharing Economy?

If you've been reading or watching the news lately, you've probably heard a lot of terms getting thrown around. You might be wondering what some of them are all about. What does it mean to be "location independent"? What's a "tiny house"? What's a "minimalist"?

While some of these terms have pretty simple definitions, others are vague and still in the process of being defined. Ask different people, and you may get a different answer. This chapter provides a crash course on some of the concepts I'll be using throughout this book. We'll look at some basic categories, the buzzwords that the media has picked up, and a few more specific definitions.

Remember, other writers may define these terms differently, and there's a lot of overlap between these categories. Often, people who are involved in one aspect of these communities may have an interest in others as well.

Collaborative Consumption

One of the most common terms that you should know is the

concept of "**collaborative consumption**". It's kind of an awkward phrase, but the concept is pretty simple: Why own when you can share?

The Collaborate Consumption movement is about having *access to goods* instead of owning them. If everyone on your block owns a lawnmower,[1] for example, chances are it's sitting idle most of the time. Could you pool your landscaping resources? What if one of you "owned" a lawnmower, someone else owned a weed-whacker, and everyone in the neighborhood had access to each kind of tool when they needed it?

This is the principle behind Zipcar, a for-profit car rental company in which members essentially "subscribe" to a car via a monthly or yearly access fee. When they need a car, they swipe their card to unlock it, and rent the vehicle for $8-10/hr. Zipcar members don't have to "own" a car, but they still have access to one when they need it. This reduces their vehicle expenses, *and* results in less cars cluttering city streets.

Peer-to-Peer Marketplace

The **peer-to-peer (P2P) marketplace** takes this one step further. Instead of renting a car from a company like Zipcar, peer-to-peer websites allow you to borrow from, share with, or rent to other people in your community.

You've probably heard of Airbnb, which allows people to rent out extra bedrooms. Sites like RelayRides and Getaround allow you to rent vehicles from other car owners in your neighborhood.

Instead of a centralized marketplace, P2P websites let you connect directly with another individual.

It's true that communities have been doing things like this for ages — think of "take a book, leave a book" lending libraries — but technology allows for these transactions to be simpler and easier than ever. Many people have smartphones that allow them to easily update their calendar when their car or extra bedroom is available for rent. Some services even match travelers going in the same direction to let them share rides.

With P2P websites, you can sell your artwork directly to customers, sign up for dinner with a local chef, or rent a neighbor's vehicle. Most of the time, you'll pay directly through the website with your credit card, meaning no awkward negotiations when you meet in person.

The Sharing Economy

The **"Sharing Economy"** is another buzzword that means different things to different people. In the past, it's been used to refer to neighborhood time-banks and other off-line communities (more on that later).

Recently, it's been used as an umbrella term that's more or less inter-changeable with Collaborative Consumption and the P2P Marketplace. Some technology companies — such as Lyft and Taskrabbit — have embraced the term, even though they don't technically involve "sharing".

In its current usage, the "Sharing Economy" refers to everything from non-profit collectives in which members share goods at no cost, to Silicon Valley-tech companies with highly-paid executives and hundreds of employees. Some people have criticized these companies like for being too corporate and profit-driven, while others, like Airbnb, have made efforts to work with local regulators and give back to the community.

Minimalism

Related to these concepts, though not directly connected, is a lifestyle movement called **minimalism**. Bloggers like Josh and Ryan at TheMinimalists.com have inspired people to live with less "stuff", de-cluttering their lives both physically and mentally.

Minimalists range in age and lifestyle, including Colin Wright, who owns so few possessions he can move from one country to another whenever he chooses, to Joshua Becker, who lives with his wife and kids in Arizona ("We are just your typical middle-class family," he writes[2] "minus the dog and physical possessions.") In both cases, they've found that life experiences are more rewarding than owning lots of things.

Likewise, Dave and Sheryl Bathrop reduced their expenses and embraced minimalism when their kids left the nest — and blog about it at Simple Life Reboot — while Debbie Well and Sam Harrington took a "gap year" in their 60s to travel the world.

Some people have taken minimalism even further, building

their own **tiny houses** that allow them to live rent-free and with low utility expenses. We're talking very small (totaling around around 80-120 sq/ft), just large enough for one or two residents. Ethan Waldman, a young entrepreneur, built his own tiny house in Vermont, while Dee Williams, a middle-aged woman looking for a change in lifestyle, lives in tiny house in Olympia, Wa.

Intentional Communities

Another way that some people are reducing expenses is by forming an **intentional community**. Intentional communities may buy food in bulk, cook group dinners, and participate in community activism or gardening projects. Unlike the rural communes of the 60s, many intentional communities are located in urban environments, including Synchronicity and the LA Eco-Village near downtown Los Angeles. The Fellowship for Intentional Community maintains a database of hundreds of similar groups all over the world.

For millennials who can't afford to buy a house of their own, an intentional community can be a great way to live in a large, spacious house without taking on a huge mortgage. Some communities are organized around lifestyle choices (such as a passion for bicycling, or a particular dietary restriction), while others are just a group of friends who choose to live together.

Intentional communities aren't just for young people. A similar concept, called **co-housing**, is especially popular with older and retiring adults. In a co-housing community, each resident may have their own apartment, but share a kitchen and other common areas with their neighbors. Many families choose to raise their kids in a co-housing environment so they can have the support of other residents to help care for them.

Lifestyle Design

Lifestyle design is a growing movement popular among freelancers and entrepreneurs. Rather than following a typical career path, some people decide upon the kind of life they want to live (say, they want to travel year-round) and they build a business model around those preferences.

The rise of niche websites and online communities means that many people can make a living blogging and consulting about the subjects they love most. Those who are able to work from anywhere — that is, they can manage their business from their laptop anywhere in the world — are said to be "**location independent**" or a "**digital nomad**". Popular sites in this category include Location 180 and the Suitcase Entrepreneur.

Often, these bloggers will gravitate toward regions of the world with a low cost of living, such as South America or Southeast Asia, where they can live for months on a tight budget. They may be involved in "**travel hacking**" — accumulating airline miles and credit card points so they can travel cheaply and get free plane flights and hotel upgrades. The Art of Non-Conformity and the Travel Hacking Cartel are popular sites in this category.

Sites Mentioned

TheMinimalists.com
ExileLifestyle.com
BecomingMinimalist.com
SimpleLifeReboot.com
GapYearAfterSixty.com
TheTinyHouse.net
PADTinyHouses.com
Ic.org (Fellowship for Intentional Community)
SynchronicityLA.com
LAEcoVillage.org
SeanOgle.com
SuitcaseEntrepreneur.com
ChrisGuillebeau.com
TravelHacking.org

Tips

*If you're looking to make a major life change, don't feel pressured to start all at once! Ryan Nicodemus, of The Minimalists, started out by packing his possessions into boxes, and seeing what he actually "needed" to unpack over thirty days. Whatever he didn't need, he threw out or gave away.

*Travel hacking can be a great way to earn free hotel rooms and airline miles. It can also be a great way to get yourself into debt. Don't take out credit cards to earn points only to find yourself stuck with annual fees and high interest rates! Do the math ahead of time.

*Not sure if you could live in an intentional community or a tiny house? Start off by visiting one for a day or a week. In the next chapter, you'll learn how to find unique places to stay on Couchsurfing and Airbnb.

---

[1] http://unlikelyradical.com/how-to-defeat-the-lawn-mower-army/
[2] http://www.becomingminimalist.com/about-us/

Travel & Homesharing

After graduating from college, I took several road-trips across the country. I rode horses in Montana, drove through parts of Canada, and explored dozens of cities and national parks. In all that time, I hardly ever stayed in a traditional hotel.

In many of the places I've visited, a local has offered to show me around town or meet up for lunch. I'm usually able to find affordable (sometimes even free) accommodations in any city that I pass through. How did I make this happen? By trusting strangers.

CouchSurfing

The global travel community changed dramatically in the early 2000's with the launch of CouchSurfing, a network for travelers and adventurers all over the world. Members of the site can offer to host guests in their own home, or request a place to stay when they're on the road.

CouchSurfing was one of the first trust-based community sites. Members could have their names or addresses verified, and could be "vouched for" by other people in the community. After meeting up with another member in person, you could leave them a review or reference.

The website became a hub for international travelers, and members could host tours, meet-up events, and other activities via regional forums. The vast majority of interactions were said to be positive; untrustworthy members were quickly weeded out.

I started out by hosting guests at my apartment in LA, to build up some karma and positive references from the community. Then, when I hit the road, I sent out a handful of requests to hosts along the way. Many of them were happy to host me and show me around town.

Why? They enjoyed sharing their perspective on their city with a visitor like me. For many people without the opportunity to travel themselves, hosting guests can be a way to travel vicariously; maybe their guest will bring a gift or cook them a traditional dish from their hometown.

I haven't used CouchSurfing in several years now, so I can't be sure that it's still the vibrant community that it used to be. It recently became a for-profit company, which some users are unhappy about. If you join, be sure to check out the profiles and reviews of anyone who requests to stay with you or offers you a couch.

Reading references thoroughly will give you a sense of which members would be a good fit for your home, or who would be a good host for you to stay with. Remember, you can always turn down requests that don't seem like a good match, or don't have any references from the community.

As an alternative, you can check out Hostelling International, which provides a similar vibe, in a more structured environment. When I traveled across Canada, I stayed in a "caboose" hostel in British Columbia, with a groups of French tourists on a cross-country camping adventure.

Airbnb

While CouchSurfing was perfect for my first few years of travel, my current go-to site for accommodations is Airbnb. Airbnb is a peer-to-peer marketplace for spare rooms and living spaces — essentially, a do-it-yourself bed-and-breakfast platform.

Like other peer-to-peer sites, hosts and guests are expected to leave reviews in order to build up a reputation in the community. Unlike CouchSurfing, accommodations aren't free. Hosts set a nightly or weekly rate, and guests request a booking via an easy-to-use calendar.

Airbnb appeals to everyone from cost-conscious travelers to well-to-do businessmen. Offerings range from the low-end (an air mattress in someone's living room) to the more upscale — highly-priced luxury townhouses and vacation getaways.

Each listing will tell you what to expect: whether pets are allowed, how to get around the neighborhood, and whether or not you'll have a private room or a shared space. Some locations are run like short-term hostels, others like monthly sublets.

What many people like about the service is that every listing is unique: instead of staying in a generic hotel, you'll get a local's-eye-view of the place you're visiting. It's also a great way to get a feel for a city that you're thinking of moving to.

For me, hosting guests via Airbnb was almost more fun than traveling. For nearly a year, my friends and I hosted guests at our house near downtown Los Angeles. Our listing was for a simple air mattress in a private room — $40 per night — and it was the perfect price point for our guests. Many of them were visiting from Europe, Australia, or other parts of the U.S. Some turned into long-term friends or acquaintances, and a few extended their stay or returned for another visit.

If you're thinking of putting up a listing, be sure to look up the laws in your city. Some places have regulations on short-term sublets, and you may be expected to pay hotel taxes on your earnings. We made several thousand dollars during our year of hosting, which helped to off-set the cost of rent and utilities. For some struggling home-owners, it's allowed them to keep their homes in the face of foreclosure.

If you're not sure what to charge or how to describe your apartment, e-mail customer service for their input. You can even ask them to send a professional photographer to take pictures of your house and improve the look of your listing.

Guests only receive your address and contact information if you approve a booking. Airbnb has a Trust & Safety team to prevent fraud or theft, and they insure hosts against property damage for up to $1 million. Still, you'll want to read the reviews of potential guests and trust your instincts if anyone seems sketchy.

A new service called Guesty will manage your bookings for a small fee, and even arrange for a cleaning service to visit your apartment between guests. KeyCafe lets you arrange for a secure key-drop at a local business, so guests can gain access to your apartment when you're away.

More Kinds of Rentals

Other companies are adding their own spin to the Airbnb model. Breather allows you to rent meeting rooms and office spaces by the hour or day — perfect if you need a quiet room to get some work done or meet with a client.

Roomi is a smartphone app that helps you look for a long-term roommate, while Crashdwell is a NY-based service specifically for students and recent college grads. ApartmentList and Zumper hope to improve the apartment-hunting process.

You can even rent out boats — with a captain or on your own — at sites like GetMyBoat, Boaterfly, Boatbound, and Cruzin. And StowThat, currently based in Seattle, lets people rent our extra storage space in their home or garage.

Sites Mentioned

CouchSurfing.org
HiHostels.com
Airbnb.com
Guesty.com
KeyCafe.com
Breather.com
Roomiapp.com
Crashdwell.com
ApartmentList.com
Zumper.com
GetMyBoat.com
Boaterfly.com
Boatbound.co
Cruzin.com
StowThat.com

Tips

* Whether you're a guest or a host, remember
you're dealing with an individual, not a business
hosts will respond to booking requests promptl
others may take some time to get back to you o
have further questions.

* Most hosts and guests mean well. Don't blo
misunderstandings out of proportion, especia
involve cultural differences.

* Put a detailed profile together as soon as you sign up for the site. People want to know who they're hosting (or staying with), so include a picture and some biographical information. Your contact info and address will only be shared when you complete a booking.

* If you're hosting, don't be afraid to ask for more information. If someone's profile is empty or they don't have a clear photo, politely ask them to fill it out before accepting their booking.

* When you request a booking, remember to include the purpose of your visit: "Hi! I'm a student from Germany traveling to the U.S. for the first time. I'm looking for a place to stay in New York from January 12-18th. Your place looks perfect! Is it available during those dates?"

* If your booking requests are declined, try a different hosts. Some hosts really are overwhelmed with requests. If you're turned down because you don't have any reviews, see if a friend who uses the site can write you a reference.

* Don't forget to factor in any taxes or fees when making a booking. If you're an Airbnb host, you may be expected to pay hotel taxes, or at the very least report the income on your personal tax return.

Rentals & Carsharing

Have you ever had a bad experience with a taxi? Maybe you waited for an hour and it never showed up, or the taxi driver was reckless and took you for a roundabout ride. How about car rentals? Waiting in line at the airport is never fun, especially when you add in all the hidden fees.

Several recent services are hoping to change that experience. By tapping into new technology, these companies are hoping to make transportation more efficient, by letting people rent each other's cars, offer rides to each other, and match riders going in the same direction.

Ridesharing

Ridesharing itself is nothing new; people have been hitchhiking for decades. More recently, people have taken to message boards like Craigslist to find passengers who can chip in for gas. Now, it's easier than ever, thanks to GPS tracking and smartphone apps.

Some sites, like Ridejoy apply the Couchsurfing model to transportation, in which passengers are only expected to cover gas. Others have turned it into a profit-based business, hiring drivers to provide on-demand rides to consumers.

On-demand services in the U.S. include Lyft, Sidecar, Hitch, and Bandwagon, all of which have similar business models, but with slight differences. Lyft encourages passengers to sit in the front seat and chat with their drivers; Sidecar lets drivers set their own fares; and Hitch and Bandwagon pair you with other riders headed in the same direction to reduce the price.

You might have heard about protests going on in major cities (especially in Europe) surrounding these businesses. Some drivers claim they're underpaid, while traditional taxi drivers worry that these services are (illegally) cutting into their market.

It's true that these rideshare services are essentially unlicensed taxis, although many of these sites have been working with regulators in order to expand their reach to more and more cities. It's unlikely they'll be going away any time soon.

Users of these services feel that they're safer and more convenient than taxis. You can look on your smartphone to see when your car will arrive, you can pay with a credit card directly through the app, and you can rate and review your driver once you arrive at your destination. Didn't like a driver? You won't be paired with them again. If a driver receives too many bad reviews, they'll be removed from the system altogether.

Services like these serve as a full- or -part-time income stream for many drivers. If your car meets the requirements and you have a good driving record, you can apply to be an driver for one of these companies. You're essentially able to set your own hours; you just log into smartphone app when you want to be on-call, and you'll be notified through the app when a customer requests a ride.

Many drivers enjoy the job, and use it to supplement their income by working during peak traffic times, or on nights and weekends. Some services claims their drivers can make up to $35/hr, though many reports have disputed that. You'll have to pay for your own gas and maintenance, so be sure to factor that in before deciding whether or not it's a good fit for you.

Car Rentals

Just as ridesharing services are disrupting the taxi industry, several new car rental companies are challenging Hertz and Enterprise. We already discussed Zipcar in the Introduction, so let's take a look at a similar service called Car2Go.

Car2Go's are super-compact, 2-passenger Smart cars, intended primarily for local trips; some cities even have an all-electric option. Like Zipcar, you'll pay a monthly membership fee, and can gain access to a car at any time by swiping your membership card across a built-in card reader.

Cars are parked curbside, so no need to go to a special location to pick it up; you can look at a smartphone app to see which one is closest to you. Car2Go charges by the minute, not mile, so it's especially convenient if you need to make a short trip to the grocery store or a doctor's appointment.

Another option is a peer-to-peer car rental service like RelayRides or Getaround. These sites allow you to rent a car directly from a car owner in your neighborhood. If you need an SUV for a camping trip, or to shop at IKEA, you can rent one by the hour or day.

I've used both sites to rent out my own SUV to locals and tourists. Since I commute by bike, and don't need my car on a daily basis, it's available for both short- and long-term rentals. I earn around $400-500 per month — enough to cover my car loan and insurance.

Here are a few things to consider when deciding which site to list your car on.

RelayRides is a better option for medium- and long-term trips. I currently list my car for around $30/day, with RelayRides taking 1/4 of the price as a booking fee. I cap my mileage allotment at 100mi/day so that renters don't put too much wear-and-tear on the vehicle.

I always ask prospective renters where they plan to go before accepting a booking. If they're just commuting around town, I'm happy to let them rent it for a few weeks at a time, with a weekly mileage allotment of 350. (If they go over the mileage limit, they're charged .75c per additional mile.) I'm less comfortable with long-distance trips, because I'd like to be nearby in case the vehicle needs any maintenance.

RelayRides verifies the identity and driving record of all renters, so I know my car is in good hands. They also insure the car for up to $1 mil on top of my own insurance policy, and they transfer my earnings directly to my bank account 3 days after a completed trip.

Getaround offers a similar service, but in my experience, it's a bit less user-friendly. The website is clunkier and the booking calendar is harder to read. They don't allow car owners to adjust the mileage limit (200/day), and their overage rate is only .40c per mile. They take a 40% cut, and they only pay out once per month via Paypal, which is a long time to wait for your earnings and adds an extra step to the process.

However, they do have an option for hourly rentals, which might be more profitable for some car owners, and they have an option of installing a card reader so that you don't have to meet up with each renter to exchange keys.

Still feeling uneasy at the prospect of renting out your car? I recommend buying a GPS tracker, so that you know where your car is at any given time. Automatic Link is one option. For around $100, you'll be sent a device that you can plug into your car's dashboard. Once it's activated, you can use a smartphone app to locate the car, compare mileage stats, and even see whether the

Check Engine light is on.

I use a device from MetroMile, which serves the same purpose. Currently, MetroMile is only available in CA, WA, OR, and IL, but they're offering some users a free GPS tracker in return for signing up for their beta program. Check it out if you're in one of those states.

More Rental Options

While carsharing is the most popular form of peer-to-peer transportation, your options don't stop there. Spinlister allows you to rent (or rent out) bikes, skis, and snowboards by the hour or day. In San Francisco, Scoot offers a scooter rental program similar to Car2Go.

Some cities are rolling out low-cost bike-sharing programs, such as CitiBike in NYC, Divvy Bikes in Chicago, or NiceRide in Minneapolis. Each of these offer the option of annual or short-term memberships, with rides under 30 minutes virtually free.

You can also rent out other things besides vehicles: CameraLends is a peer-to-peer camera rental service, ShareHammer lets you rent out tools, and ParkCirca lets share your driveway (currently only in SF). GearCommons lets you rent canoes, tents, and other outdoor gear. If your city hasn't caught on to these concepts yet, start spreading the word and maybe one of these companies will launch in your area next!

Sites Mentioned

Ridejoy.com
Lyft.me
Side.cr
TakeHitch.com
BandWagon.io
Zipcar.com
Car2Go.com
RelayRides.com
Getaround.com
MetroMile.com
Automatic.com
Spinlister.com
CitiBike.com
DivvyBikes.com
NiceRideMN.org
CameraLends.com
ShareHammer.com
ParkCirca.com
GearCommons.com

Tips

* As with homesharing sites, make sure to fill out your profile in advance of making a booking. Any car rental sites will want to verify your driving history, so have

your driver's license handy when you sign up.

* When requesting a rental, include some details about your trip: "Hi Jake. We're a family of four visiting Austin for the weekend. We won't be traveling too far, but we'd love to borrow your SUV to check out some hiking trails nearby. Looks like it gets great gas mileage!"

* If you're renting out your car, you'll be able to set mileage limits and adjust the hourly, daily, or weekly rate. Try out different price points and see which rate gets you the most cost-effective rentals. Remember that the service in question will be taking a cut of your profits.

* When meeting up with a renter, check their drivers license and make sure it matches the name on the reservation. Let them know any relevant info about your car and take photos of any damages. Note your odometer and gas level, and remind them to refill the tank before they return the car.

* You don't always have to be present for pick-up and drop-off. Some services have high-tech devices that let you leave your key in a lock-box attached to the vehicle. Or, you can leave the key at a designated place at your house.

* Try to do a spot-check and basic clean of your car between renters. They won't expect it to be spotless, but it should be reasonably well-kept.

* Are you able to do airport pick-ups and drop-offs? Offer to meet your renter at a convenient location for an extra tip.

Meals & Experiences

Do you enjoy cooking, but can't stand cooking for yourself? Maybe you're a college grad living a new city, and are tired of having the same old dinner every night after work. Or maybe you're a parent with no one to cook for now that the kids have moved out.

Eating dinner doesn't have to be lonely. Just as Airbnb reinvented the hotel experience, several new websites are hoping to change the way that we cook and share food. From swapping leftovers to hosting dinners in your home, here are a few ways you can get in on the action.

Mealsharing

For college grads who have grown up using CouchSurfing and similar sites, sharing meals with strangers seems like the logical next step. Why eat alone when you could be connecting with colleagues, neighbors, and visitors from all over the world?

"A lot of people say, 'That's crazy, I would never do that,'" said Brian Chesky, CEO of Airbnb, during a talk at the Aspen Ideas Summit.[1] "But ask you kids if they would do that — and they probably would."

The most straightforward site of the bunch is called Mealsharing, and it's as simple as it sounds. Members post an image and description of the meal they plan to cook, the number of seats available, and the date and time. Other members can request to join them for dinner.

The website offers some tips for hosts ("No need to worry about making an over the top gourmet meal. It's more about sharing and good conversation.") and guests ("Whether a great story or a bottle of wine, bring something along to show your appreciation."). As with any of these sites, members have the option to review a positive experience, or flag a negative one.

A step up from Mealsharing are sites like Feastly, Eatwith, and NewGusto which offer a similar experience, for a moderate fee. Hosts are more likely to have some experience as cooks, and may offer more elaborate menus.

Here are a sample of meals available on Feastly: Taco Tuesday in South Miama, FL for $12/person. A 3-course Italian dinner in Baltimore for $35/person. A "family style Persian dinner" in Chicago for $40/person.

Don't be scared off by the fancy menus. A meal can be as formal or as casual as you want it to be. Hosts cook and serve the dinner in their own homes, so they can set the tone of the evening and let guests know what to expect.

Do you have a favorite Paleo or vegan dish that you'd like to share? Maybe a traditional menu item you family makes? See if you can ask a few friends to help out for the evening to take some of the pressure off.

It's up to you how much you want to charge for the meal. For some amateur cooks, hosting dinners can be a steady side-income. Even if you're not in it to make a profit, at the very least you can expect to earn back the cost of ingredients.

Other Foodsharing Services

Maybe hosting guests in your home is a bit much for you. Sites like LeftoverSwap and ShareYourMeal allow you to exchange your leftover food for free. If you're always cooking more than you can eat, consider listing the extra portions online for your neighbors to pick up.

Eatro and Mealku take it a step further by letting you turn your love of cooking into a part-time business. You can set aside portions of your favorite stir-fry for pick-up, or charge a small fee for delivery. You can try something new each time, or stick to one of your classic recipes.

These sites are still rolling out and building momentum, so if they aren't available in your city yet, see if you can find one that is. Maybe you can organize your neighbors and start a local foodsharing group of your own.

Others services include NeighborhoodFruit, which lets you invite your neighbors to pick fruit from your yard, and MyCityGardens (Boston only), which helps gardeners find plots of land to share.

Tours and Experiences

Sharing food is one of the best ways to welcome people to your neighborhood or explore a new city or culture, but it's not the only option. Vayable lets you offer tours to individuals or small groups. Guests get to experience the city "as a local," and see a side of things that they wouldn't find on a traditional bus tour.

In Portland, you can choose from a tour of local food carts, a hike in the Columbia River Gorge, or a guided drive along the coast. In LA, you can go on a 32-mile bike tour, a "Magical Malibu Adventure," and more.

There are several similar services — including SideTour, CanaryHop, and GetYourGuide — so find out which one is most popular in your area. Even if you're not an expert on your city, don't worry. What matters is that you know your way around and you're excited about living here!

Maybe you have an inside view of an arts scene or neighborhood that most visitors don't get to experience. Maybe your friends tell you that you're a passionate advocate for your city. Why not create a tour of your own and share that perspective?

As with any of these services, you can set the price and date/time that your tour will be available, and you can decline guests whom you don't think would be a good fit. Remember to encourage guests to leave a review if they've enjoyed your tour!

Sites Mentioned

Mealsharing.com

EatFeastly.com

Eatwith.com

NewGusto.com

Eatro.com

Mealku.com

NeighborhoodFruit.com

MyCityGardens.com

Vayable.com

SideTour.com

CanaryHop.com

GetYourGuide.com

Tips

* The same tips that apply to car and home sharing apply here. Always fill our your profile beforehand, be as specific as possible with any requests, and leave a review of your meal or experience after it's complete.

* For some sites, you'll need to have a menu and some pictures of a meal you've made before you can list an event. For tours and experiences, you may need to record a short video introducing yourself and your

offering.

* Whether you're a host or a guest, be sensitive to other cultures and traditions. Don't sign up for a meal without reading the menu thoroughly. If you have any dietary restrictions, ask beforehand if they can be accommodated.

* Some cities have restrictions on how many dinner parties you can host before being an "unlicensed restaurant". Be aware of and abide by any health codes that exist in your area.

---

[1] http://www.aspenideas.org/session/airbnb-how-sharing-economy-redefining-marketplace-and-our-sense-community

Gigs & Services

The world of work is changing. In the past, a skilled employee could expect to remain with the same company for decades, making their way up the ladder. Partly because of the economic downturn, and partly because of technological changes, companies are cutting back on full-time employees, and more people are working as freelancers or starting their own small businesses.

According to the Freelancers Union, nearly 42 million Americans are working "as freelancers, temps, 'permalancers', perma-temps, contractors, contingent workers, etc."[1] The number is only likely to rise in the near future, creating even more competition for stable employment.

If you've recently been laid off, or are struggling to find work out of college, here are some websites that can help you find short-term gigs. Whether you enjoy temp work, are looking for a full-time job, or just need some extra cash, these tools can be a great source of side-income.

TaskRabbit

When I was a struggling film school grad just out of college, I turned to a site called TaskRabbit to help me find gigs. At the time, customers would post work that they needed done, and task runners like me would "bid" on how much money we'd like to be paid to complete that particular task.

Tasks ranged from building IKEA furniture, to staffing an event or conference, to general office assistance. In some cities, task runners could pick up enough gigs to earn a full-time income. Taskrabbit recently implemented a site-wide $11.20/hr minimum wage; at the time, my own gigs averaged $10-15 per hour.

While the format of the site has changed a bit, the general idea is the same. "Taskers" are background checked freelancers with various skill sets, including office help, event management, housekeeping, and more.

Clients can hire individual Taskers by the hour, for one-time or recurring projects. Just as with other sites that we've discussed, the process is fully transparent: Clients review Taskers after the job is completed, and all of the payment and contact details are exchanged through a smartphone app.

My longest-running TaskRabbit gig was for a company called Lootcrate. They hired me directly through the TaskRabbit service, and for several days each month, I helped them pack and ship boxes to their subscribers. They had thousands of boxes to process each month, so they needed dozens of Taskers.

I got to know a lot of the other Taskers during my time there.

For many of them, short-term gigs like this one were a way to supplement their income and make ends meet. Several of the Taskers were college students or recent grads, while others were semi-retired and well over 60. As the traditional job market becomes more difficult for both young and old workers to break into, sites like TaskRabbit can be a good way to gain experience and make connections.

Other Gigs

TaskRabbit isn't the only site available for short-term work. Gigwalk is a smartphone app that pays individuals to complete tasks for local businesses. These range from taking pictures of a storefront to answering questions about inventory. You might even be sent into a store as a "mystery shopper" to make sure employees are following proper procedures.

FieldAgent hires people to audit local businesses. While you won't be paid much for each task ($3-12), many of them only take a few minutes and you could easily complete several per hour.

Sites like these are especially appealing for unemployed college grads who don't want to work in a retail or food service environment. They can set their own hours and choose their own gigs. Some are intended to help students build up a resume before they graduate.

A site called Bellhops lets people hire college students for local moving help. All of the students may wear matching headbands, but they're individually rated by customers after each gig.

In an Inc.com article, Shelley Provost writes, "Customer feedback ratings will be aggregated and released to each Bellhop upon graduating from their respective college. It's a living resume that will carry much more weight than the paper kind."[2]

More Services

In New York and San Francisco, a site called Postmates hires temp workers to deliver items from local restaurants and stores. Don't have a car? You can sign up to deliver by bike or scooter. A service called InstaCart offers on-demand grocery delivery. Customers use the site to create a shopping list, and on-the-ground shoppers are paid to purchase and deliver the items. Shoppers can earn up to $25/hour.

While these gigs may not be what you imagined doing with your college degree, or in your retirement years, for some people they have a strong appeal. You can book gigs on the go, right then and there, using your smartphone. You don't have to schedule weeks in advance, or go through a lengthy interview process only to be turned down. Your reputation and references will carry with you if you move to a new city.

Plus, there are so many options out there that chances are you can find something you enjoy doing. UrbanSitter will connect you with local families in need of babysitting help. Sites like Rover and DogVacay hire you to walk or take care of dogs in your own home for an hourly or daily rate.

Over the holidays, I had the chance to dogsit for a local pet-owner who was going out of town. Since I'm not able to have a pet of my own, it was a great opportunity to have some company for the week and earn some extra cash.

All of these sites have protections in place to guarantee the safety of everyone involved, such as an emergency hot-line if the pet that you're caring for gets sick. They'll even insure you in the case of property damage or injury.

For pet owners, a peer-to-peer service can be a great alternative to leaving your dog in an overcrowded kennel. You can find a personalized dog-sitter who will text you with updates and send you pictures of your pet. For pet-lovers, it can be a fun part-time gig.

More and more services are launching every year. If you have experience with house cleaning or repairs, you might consider looking for gigs on Zaarly, Homejoy, or Handybook. A new site called Favor offers on-demand delivery in Austin and Boston. Alfred Club is a kind of subscription-based TaskRabbit, offering shopping, cleaning, and delivery services to members on a recurring basis.

Sites Mentioned

TaskRabbit.com

GigWalk.com

FieldAgent.net

GetBellhops.com

Postmates.com

Instacart.com

UrbanSitter.com

Rover.com

DogVacay.com

Zaarly.com

Homejoy.com

Handybook.com

FavorDelivery.com

AlfredClub.com

Tips

* It can be especially tricky to negotiate with clients for short-term gigs. Don't work for less than you're worth, but be aware that many users of these sites are looking for a bargain. It's up to you to insist on a fair rate.

* Your client may not think of a TaskRabbit or DogVacay host as a "professional". Remind them that you've been vouched for and background-checked by the site in question. If you have any relevant credentials or degrees, go ahead and list them on your profile.

* Always work by the hour when possible. That way, if a gig takes longer than expected, you'll be paid accordingly, and aren't stuck with a flat rate.

* If you do settle on a flat rate, make sure you have all the information you need to price it fairly. How many hours do you expect it to take? Will lunch or transportation be included? Your client is likely to underestimate the work involved, so have a plan in case it goes substantially over.

* Remember that the site in question will deduct a fee for every transaction. Factor that in before agreeing on a rate.

* If you're hosting a pet, don't skip the meet-and-greet beforehand. You'll want to make sure that the pet feels at home in your house or yard before agreeing to care for it for any length of time.

---

[1] http://www.theguardian.com/commentisfree/cifamerica/2012/feb/07/how-america-became-nation-freelancers
[2] http://www.inc.com/shelley-prevost/5-ways-to-create-more-autonomy-at-work.html

Freelancing & Consulting

What if you want to offer a product or service that's unique to you? You don't see yourself as just another taskrunner or gigwalker — you have experience with a particular skill or craft, and you want customers to know where to find you.

Maybe you're a copywriter, a video editor, or a graphic designer. Maybe you're a nutritionist, a life coach, or a yoga instructor. Whatever your skill set, finding clients via the Internet can be easier than ever. Here are some websites that cater specifically to freelancers and consultants.

Freelance Websites

We discussed TaskRabbit in the previous chapter. Even if you aren't interested in handyman and delivery tasks, you can list other skills on your TaskRabbit profile. I've landed dozens of video editing gigs through TaskRabbit, many of which I could work on from home.

TaskRabbit allows you to set an hourly rate for your specialized services, and clients can browse your profile and contact you through the website to offer you a gig. You'll get paid through the site when you're finished, so you may never even meet the client in person.

There are dozens of similar websites that can help you find freelance work. Fiverr is a community for low-budget creative gigs, such as graphic design and marketing help. While you won't be able to earn a lot of money, if you have a service that you can do quickly and easily — such as recording a short voice-over, or making tweaks to a Photoshop image — you might be able to speed through several tasks in an hour.

Elance and ODesk are mid-range freelance sites, specializing in internet technology, copywriting, translation services, and more. As with most of the sites in this section, you'll be able to work remotely. The downside is that you'll be competing with freelancers from all over the world (many of whom will work for lower rates than you), so you'll want to create a great profile with samples of your work to stand out from the crowd.

Higher-end freelance sites include CoWorks, which focuses on creative and artistic services, and Skillbridge, for business and marketing work.

Teaching & Consulting

If you're more interested in on-on-one teaching or consulting, you can list your offerings on a site specific to your niche. Maybe you're a yoga teacher looking to offer private lessons. A profile on YogaTrail can help you reach out to students and connect with other instructors. Your students can even leave you a review if they enjoyed your lesson.

Recently, Google launched a program called Helpouts, in which experts offer online help sessions via video chats. You can set your own price per hour or minute, or offer a free initial session as a way to a attract clients.

There are several similar services out there. Clarify.fm offers one-on-one calls with experts over the phone. MicroMentor sets up ongoing mentorship arrangements with aspiring artists and entrepreneurs.

What about teaching an online course? If you have a lesson plan in mind that you think would be helpful to people, you can apply to offer it on Skillshare. If accepted, you'll create written and/or video lessons in advance, so you don't need to be there in person to teach the class. Students interact with you via the website, and you can give them feedback on their homework and class assignments.

Getting Paid

Most of these sites pay you directly, so you never have to worry about late invoices or bounced checks. But what happens if you find a client offline? How can you ensure that you get paid promptly?

I like to use online invoicing tools, which let me e-mail an invoice directly to a client. Your client will be able to pay you via credit card or online transfer, minus a small fee for the transaction. I currently use Wave for invoicing, but some freelancers prefer Freshbooks or Outright. Many of these services offer bookkeeping options, so you can keep track of all your business profits and expenses.

Another option is to get a credit-card reader for your iPad or iPhone. You've probably seen these at many cafes and restaurants. It's an easy, hassle-free alternative to cash or check. A popular service is Square, although many other card readers are also available.

If you teach yoga, for example, you can ask your student to pay by credit card before or after class. You'll just swipe the credit card via the reader (or manually type in the credit card number), and your student or client can sign directly on the screen.

When you earn income from many sources, you'll want to keep good records for tax purposes. Check out 1099.is for some tips on filing taxes as an independent contractor. Also, you may want to have a few contracts on hand for working with clients. A contract can stipulate when and how you'll be paid, and what work is expected of you during a given project. Shake is a smartphone app that helps you create simple, legally-binding contracts for all kinds of projects.

Sites Mentioned

CoWorks.com
SkillBridge.co

Fiverr.com
Elance.com
ODesk.com
YogaTrail.com
Skillshare.com
Helpouts.Google.com
Clarity.fm
Waveapps.com
Freshbooks.com
Outright.com
Square.com
1099.is
ShakeLaw.com

Tips

* If you're going into freelance consulting, see if you can offer several practice sessions pro-bono before taking on a paying client. You don't want to freeze up under the pressure of your first big Skype call.

* Ask your first clients if they'd be willing to write a testimonial or give you feedback in return for their consultation. Several good testimonials on your website can be the key to landing more clients. Make sure to include a photo with each testimonial — it really makes a difference!

* Get familiar with the technical details too. Skype and Google Hangouts are notorious for connectivity issues, and you don't want to spend half of the session just trying to get your camera or microphone to work.

* It's generally a good idea to wear headphones during Skype calls, so that you don't get feedback through your built-in speakers. If you can, record the audio of your session as a bonus for your client.

* Different types of coaching and consultations have different certification requirements. Don't claim to be something that you're not, and include any relevant disclaimers on your website. Consult with a lawyer if necessary.

* Do your research before paying for any fancy credentials. Planning to be a life coach? You'll probably want to get certified. Helping people based on your own personal or business experiences? Probably not necessary.

* It's up to you whether to request payment before or after a consultation. (I suggest before.) For long-term freelance projects — such as web design or copywriting — it's a good idea to request half up front and the rest upon delivery of the finished product.

Blogs & Storefronts

You've probably heard stories about people who make a living blogging. Some of them blog from the road and earn a full-time income at it. There are dozens of ways to make money as a blogger, from selling products or e-books, to affiliate advertising and sponsorship, to writing paid articles for other blogs.

It takes a lot of time to build up an audience, so don't expect to get rich off of blogging anytime soon. But if you work at it consistently, promote your work well, and connect with your readers, you might be able to build a business out of it.

Here are a few blogging platforms and online storefronts for you to consider.

Blog Platforms

Blogs range from the simple (Tumblr and Blogger are among the most popular) to highly customizable and complex. You'll probably want to start off somewhere in the middle. Weebly and Wix both offer free or cheap blogging options to get you started.

Once you've signed up, you'll be able to pick a theme, and drag-and-drop photos and text to get the design you're looking for. A typical blog will include an About page, a Contact page, and a mailing list sign-up form. You should also include links to your social media profiles on Twitter or Facebook.

If you're looking for a more advanced blogging platform, I recommend Squarespace. It's a bit pricier ($8/month), but it has an easy-to-use interface and great customer support. Any time I have a question or need help, I can expect a response in less than half an hour.

Blogs can be a bit tricky to get started, so don't stress out. There are plenty of free resources to get you rolling. Remember, it takes a long time to build up an audience, so don't expect lots of readers overnight. It may take a year or more before you start to see results.

One way that you can grow your readership is by using a mailing list. Mailchimp and Madmimi are two free or low-cost options. People who want to receive updates will provide you with their e-mail address, and you can e-mail the entire group whenever you have an announcement.

You can also promote your blog via social media. Programs like Buffer and Hootsuite automate your posts so you can share updates regularly without being online all day. Just set the times that you want your content to be posted, and these services will share them automatically. Buffer also has a great blog with helpful tips on how to manage your social media accounts.

Storefronts

Internet commerce is bigger than ever. In the old days, people were afraid to enter their credit card numbers online. Now, it's the way many people do most of their shopping. If you have a product or service that you can offer alongside your blog, you're on your way to running your own online business.

One popular service is Shopify. With a Shopify account, you'll be able to create a list of inventory (T-shirts, prints of your artwork, or whatever it is that you sell), and be notified when you receive an order. Shopify processes the customer's credit card, and you ship the item to their address.

Many ecommerce sites can be integrated with a shipping service that will take care of packaging and shipping for you. For example, you can link your Shopify store with Shipwire and automate the entire process.

Other types of online storefronts allow you to sell designs for T-shirts, iPhone cases, and more. All you do is upload the image to the site, and they'll print and ship the item when someone places an order. No need to buy lots of shirts up front, only to find them sitting in your garage when nobody buys them. Popular print-on-demand services include CafePress, Zazzle, and Redbubble.

As with any store, you're going to have to do a lot of work to promote and sell your products. Only a few people get lucky and sell thousands of dollars of items all at once. Your profit margin will depend on what you're selling, and how well you advertise.

If you've built up an audience for your blog, or have lots of followers on social media, reach out to them and see what kinds of products they'd like you to offer. If your Instagram photos are popular, for example, you could list them on Twenty20, which sells prints and iPhone cases.

People want to feel as though they're buying from a real person. It's important to build up a relationship with your customers by answering their questions, thanking them for their purchase, and asking them to spread the word about your products.

More Resources

This chapter was only a quick overview, so I want to make sure you have some follow-up resources if this is something you're interested in pursuing. Two popular books that I found useful are Chris Guillebeau's *The $100 Startup* and Tim Ferriss's *The Four-Hour Workweek*. Both of these books will give you some ideas to get you started, as well as more detailed information about the logistics of running an online business.

Don't let the sheer number of options overwhelm you. The best way to get started is to pick something and try it out! If it doesn't work, try something else until you find the system that works for you. We'll talk more about these concepts in the chapter on Entrepreneurship.

Sites Mentioned

Wix.com
Weebly.com
Squarespace.com
Mailchimp.com
Madmimi.com
Bufferapp.com
Hootsuite.com
Shopify.com
Shipwire.com
CafePress.com
Zazzle.com
Redbubble.com
Twenty20.com

Tips

* Building an audience for your blog will take time. Write consistently, and don't give up! The more content you have, the more likely you are to show up in search results and boost traffic.

* Consider writing "guest posts" for other bloggers. The more sites that link to yours, the more traffic you'll get. While you probably won't get paid for a guest post, a popular post can draw traffic for years to come.

* Another good idea is to write a "round-up" post

profiling several of your favorite bloggers. Let them know that you've included them; there's a good chance they'll be honored and share it with their audience.

* If your blog or website service doesn't come with built-in traffic stats, sign up for Google Analytics or another tool for monitoring traffic. You'll be able to see what terms your visitors are searching for, which country they're based in, and which sites referred them to yours.

* You can look at the stats for your social media accounts and mailing list too. If people aren't opening your e-mails, don't get discouraged. A 10% open-rate is pretty good, even for popular bloggers. Experiment with different subject lines and content to see what works best.

* Remember that your social media posts are likely to get buried pretty quickly. Don't be afraid to post the same thing more than once, at different times of the day, to reach a wider audience.

* Try to alternate self-promotion with other helpful content. Include useful links in your e-mails to readers. Reach out to your fans and re-Tweet content that they've shared. Follow back people who have shown an interest in your work.

Art, Music, & More

The Internet has changed the landscape for artists of all kinds. You no longer have to wait for a traditional book publisher, record label, or movie studio to get your work out. More and more artists are choosing to self-publish books, release their own albums, and sell their work directly to consumers.

In some cases, this means you can make more of a profit. Selling e-books has a higher profit margin than paperbacks, for example. But it also means you'll be competing with more people than ever, so you'll have to work really hard to stand out from the crowd and get people's attention.

One option is to look for a niche audience — people who like a very specific kind of art. Another option is to work in multiple kinds of media. If you write e-books, for example, consider turning a quote from your book into a T-shirt or an Instagram photo.

The more content you have, the easier it will be to make a living at it. Colin Wright, for example, has dozens of e-books available, teaches an online class, and runs a small publishing company. Since he works on so many different projects, he's able to appeal to a broad audience.

E-books

You've probably heard about the decline in book sales over the past decade. But did you know that e-books sales are skyrocketing, and out-pacing paperback sales by a large margin? There used to be a stigma around self-publishing, but that's changing quickly.

Why self-publish? Maybe your book is on a niche topic that won't reach a wide audience, but it would be really helpful to a small group of people. Maybe you already have a following on your blog and don't want to look for an agent to represent your work.

Traditional publishers will take a year or more to bring your book to market, and you'll only receive a small share of royalties. With e-publishing, you can get your book online instantly (which is especially important if it's on a topical subject), and you'll earn up to 70% of profits.

The most popular e-book platform is Kindle Direct Publishing, run by Amazon. You'll need to format your manuscript according to their guidelines, upload a cover image, and set the price and royalty rate. Once it's accepted, you can share the link with your friends and readers, and other people will be able to search for your book in the Kindle Store. You'll receive a monthly sales report, and any profits will be sent directly to your bank account.

This can be a tricky process, so I've *really* simplified it here. There are lots of free resources that can walk you through it, including this in-depth guide to online publishing by Asymmetrical Press.[1]

If you choose to self-publish, you'll want to make your book as professional as possible. You might consider hiring a professional editor or cover designer. If you don't have a lot of money to spend, GoOnWrite offers affordable, "pre-made" covers you can customize for your book.

You can also publish your book via Smashwords, which will distribute the book to a dozen online stores, including Kindle, Barnes & Noble, Kobo, iBooks, and more. If you'd like to offer a hard copy of your book, Createspace is a popular print-on-demand service. This means that books are only printed when someone places an order, so you don't have to stockpile — or even ship —the books yourself.

Clothes & Crafts

Online marketplaces are a great place to sell handmade goods. Many artists, fashion designers, and hand-crafters sell their work directly through Etsy, Bonanza, or Uncommon Goods. Kari Chapin has a great guide on the subject called "The Handmade Marketplace."

Other sites are tapping into the peer-to-peer model. At Thredup, you can send in your used clothing and accessories, and receive up to 80% of the sales price for any items that are accepted. There's even a price calculator on their website so you can get an estimate ahead of time of how much you're likely to make. Similar services include Twice, Poshmark, and Threadflip, all for various items and price-points.

A related marketplace for kids' clothing is Double Dutchery. Rather than ordering specific items, customers have the option of ordering a box of clothing for a particular age/size. If you have a box of quality used clothing, you can list it for sale on the site, and ship it when someone places an order.

For larger items, such as furniture and antiques, there's Krrb, which specializes in local, in-person transactions — kind of like an online yard-sale. Yerdle is the same idea, only rather than a money-based marketplace, customers buy and sell with credits.

We've come a long way since the days of Craigslist. With sites like these, you don't have to worry about who you're interacting with. Peer-to-peer marketplaces are all about transparency and repeat business, not one-time, anonymous transactions.

Music & More

What about other kinds of art, like music and video? While it's a bit harder to sell these kinds of media directly, many savvy podcasters and video bloggers have turned their projects into ongoing revenue streams. Some are so popular that they make money through ads and sponsorships by big-name companies.

You don't need a lot of time or energy to create a podcast. Dave and Sheryl Bathrop, of SimpleLifeReboot, started a podcast to share their journey toward minimalism and simple-living, and each episode is just 10-15 minutes long.

Pick a topic that interests you, and start off by interviewing people you already know. You can call up your interview subjects via Skype, and use a program like ECamm to record the audio or video. By sticking to a regular schedule and format, podcasts and video blogs can function like a radio or TV show.

Whether you're creating a podcast, a video, or a music project, you'll need a place to upload your content. Many podcasts distribute through iTunes, so listeners can download each episode directly to their smartphone. For high-end video projects, Vimeo is a popular option, while Soundcloud is a great place to upload songs.

If you have an entire album that you'd like to share, consider adding it to Bandcamp. You can set a price per track or for the whole album, or let listeners download songs for free. You can even offer CD, vinyl records, and other merchandise through the site.

Sites Mentioned

Colin.io
KDP.Amazon.com

Asymmetrical.co/how-1/
GoOnWrite.com
Smashwords.com
Createspace.com
Etsy.com
Bonanza.com
UncommonGoods.com
Thredup.com
LikeTwice.com
Poshmark.com
Threadflip.com
DoubleDutchery.com
Krrb.com
Yerdle.com
Skype.com
Ecamm.com
Vimeo.com
Soundcloud.com
Bandcamp.com

Tips

* Be *very* wary of scams in the self-publishing world. While professional editing and design services can be useful, you should *never* have to pay to publish your work. Also, don't invest too much in cover design and marketing unless you know your book can sell.

* As with any other product, experiment with price points and delivery platforms. If your e-book isn't selling, try lowering the price. $2.99-4.99 works well for many writers. For printed books, aim for $9.99.

* If you're writing a series, consider selling the first book for as little as $.99 to draw readers in, and pricing the sequels higher.

* Amazon's Kindle Select program allows you to offer your e-books for free for up to 5 days in any 90-day cycle. This is a great way to get your book in front of new readers, who might otherwise never have read it.

* Always include a link to your other work in any e-book that you publish. End your book with a thank-you note and ask your readers to share a link on Facebook or Twitter. Remind them how important reviews are, and ask them to write one.

* It should go without saying, but never review your own book on a sales platform! If you ask someone to review your book, encourage them to leave an *honest* review. 5-star reviews from friends and family don't sell books; authentic 4- and 5-star reviews do.

* Try to include several blurbs on your book cover or in the description. Ask another writer in the same genre if

they'd be willing to write one for you. Chances are they'll say yes! It's a great way for them to get their own name in front of a new audience.

---

[1] http://asymmetrical.co/how-1/

Crowdfunding & Marketing

If you haven't yet taken part in a crowdfunding campaign, there's a good chance that you've been asked to donate to one, by friends and family members, even by artists and musicians that you support. It seems like everyone's running a Kickstarter or GoFundMe campaign these days: people have raised money for personal projects, for health-related expenses, for feature films, and for music albums.

If you decided to pursue crowdfunding for your project, you'll have to work hard to stand out from the crowd. Only 44% of all Kickstarters have been successfully funded. It's a competitive market, but it continues to be a source of funding for many artists.

Crowdfunding

The traditional crowdfunding format — and by "traditional," I mean Kickstarter, which was launched in 2009 — is pretty straightforward. You'll create a profile page for your campaign outlining your fundraising goals, what the money will be spent on, and any challenges that might get in the way of completing the project.

Campaigns typically run for around a month, with most

contributors donating in the first and last few days of the campaign. On Kickstarter, only campaigns that hit their goal receive funding (of which the company takes 5%). If a campaign doesn't reach its target, donor's credit cards will not be charged.

There are lots of books on how to run a successful campaign, so we won't get into that here. At the very least, you'll want to have a thorough description of your project, and a video introducing yourself and your team. Crowdfunding sites will promote a few projects on their homepage, but mostly you'll be finding donors by tapping your personal network.

Crowdfunding campaigns generally offer rewards to their donors at various donation levels. These can range from a personal thank-you postcard for a $5 donation, to an invitation to a film screening when the project is complete. Try to tie-in your rewards to the project as much as possible. If you're raising funds for a movie, you might offer a DVD or a movie poster as a reward; for a music project, a digital download of the album.

While Kickstarter is popular for art and creative projects, other crowdfunding platforms may be more in line with your goals. Indiegogo offers a wider variety of project categories, and also has a "flexible funding model". This means that even if your campaign doesn't reach it's goal, you'll still receive funds; however, the company will take a larger cut (9% vs. 4%).

If you're looking to raise money for a personal project — say, to replace camera gear that was stolen, or to cover a personal health crisis— you'll want to try GoFundMe. If you're an entrepreneur or social changemaker, StartSomeGood may be the best option.

Crowdfunding is also popular for science-based projects. Recently, the meal-replacement drink Soylent launched a successful campaign on Tilt Open, offering shipments of the product to donors once research & development was complete.

Patronage Sites

One of the concerns that donors have raised about Kickstarter is that there isn't any way to guarantee delivery of the promised rewards, or even completion of the project. Once the money is distributed, it's out of Kickstarter's hands.

This means that a project can drag on for years without any regular updates to donors. The money could be spent up front on the production of a video, without any funds set aside for distribution. The recipient may not have enough money left over to fulfill the promised rewards.

That's why some crowdfunding services are switching to a subscription-based model, in which donors can support an artist they like in small increments, over a longer period of time. As a result, they can develop an ongoing relationship with the artist and keep track of their progress over months or years.

On Patreon, for example, donors are referred to as "patrons," and pledge a small amount of money per month or per project. Every time the artist releases a new item (an e-book, a YouTube video, a song), the donor will receive direct access to it, and they'll be charged the amount of their pledge.

With this model, the artist can depend on a consistent amount of funding for each project, rather than having to launch a new campaign each time. Some content creators earn thousands of dollars per project. Destin, of Smarter Every Day, has 1,000+ patrons contributing a total of $3,500 for each Youtube video he creates. Even if some are only contributing $1 or $2 each month, he can count on substantial support for each video.

A similar service called Tugboat allows content creators to grow their audience and develop a relationship with their fans. For a small donation, donors can gain access to an exclusive mailing list or online course, or help sponsor a podcast or blog.

More Crowdfunding Platforms

Other sites are taking the crowdfunding model in a different direction. Services like Inkshares and Unbound are a cross between a crowdfunding platform and a traditional publisher.

At Inkshares, authors submit a proposal for a project, and users of the site decide which projects they want to support. If the author hits their funding goal, Inskshares will professionally edit, design, and distribute the book to publishers.

The model is appealing to authors because they'll receive a portion of the funds in advance, even before completing the book. They can use it to do research, or take time off work to write the manuscript. Rather than spending years on a project without knowing whether it will find an audience, they've already "presold" a substantial number of copies. In addition, Inkshares promises 70% of royalties, the same amount that many self-published authors receive from Amazon.

If your ideas lean more toward scientific innovation, Quirky is a crowdfunding site for product ideas and technical inventions. Just as with some of these other platforms, you'll pitch an idea which is then voted on by the public. If it's successful, Quirky will develop the product (with your input) and bring it to market, and you'll receive a share of any sales. Previous products include flexible surge protectors and smartphone-controlled air conditioners.

If it's not money you're seeking, but awareness for an organization or cause, Thunderclap lets you crowdfund Tweets and Facebook shares. You write the message, and your contributors pledge to share it on a particular date. They'll link their social media account directly to Thunderclap, and if you receive enough support, Thunderclap will blast out the message all at once, amplifying your reach.

Affiliate Marketing

There's one more approach to building an audience that's worth mentioning. It's not quite crowdfunding, but it can amplify your outreach in a similar way. Affiliate marketing is essentially commission-based sales: if someone promotes your product, they get a percentage.

One way to incorporate affiliate marketing is to sell your product via a site like Sellfy. Your readers and fans — who presumably like the book — can sign up for an affiliate account and get a special link to share with their own followers. If anyone buys the product via their link, they get a commission.

Sellfy automates the process — you'll never have to worry about paying your affiliates directly — but you get to decide how much they earn. Don't be cheap: some businesses will offer a 51/49 share to encourage their affiliates to share the product as if it were their own.

Be careful about ethical considerations here, though. You don't want a bunch of people promoting an inferior product just because they can make a lot of money doing it. Make sure that anything you sell via an affiliate program is something you truly stand by.

Likewise, if you sign on to be an affiliate for someone else's product, you should disclose this information before sharing the link — especially if you've also positively reviewed the product in question. You don't want to create the appearance of a conflict of interest.

Consider including a disclaimer along these lines: "The links on this page may be affiliate links. I only recommend products that I use personally. Affiliate payments help keep this site running, but if you prefer not to use these links, you can go directly to Amazon to purchase these products."

Gumroad and SendOwl are similar to Sellfy, but with different pricing and affiliate marketing options.

Sites Mentioned

Kickstarter.com
Indiegogo.com
GoFundMe.com
StartSomeGood.com
Open.Tilt.com
Patreon.com
TugboatYards.com
Inkshares.com
Unbound.co.uk
Quirky.com
Thunderclap.it
Sellfy.com
Gumroad.com
SendOwl.com

Tips

* When setting a campaign goal, don't aim for an unrealistic amount of funding. If your friends and supporters are all starving artists like you, expect a bunch of small donations, rather than large ones.

* A campaign that looks close to being funded looks more appealing to donors than a struggling project. Campaigns that reach 20% of their goal have an 80%

chance of being funded. Ask your friends to donate sooner rather than later to boost the snowball effect.

* Some sites halt funding once your goal is reached; others allow you to surpass the target amount. Better to aim low and surpass your target than to aim low and have your project flop.

* Make sure that you can afford the rewards that you promise donors. If you offer branded mugs or T-shirts, have you factored in production costs and shipping? You don't want to end up in a situation where half of your funding amount goes toward fulfilling rewards.

* Keep donors updated on your progress. Even if you have a set-back, it's better to be up-front about it than to make excuses. Some donors are more interested in the creative process than the finished project. They'll enjoying hearing about your adventures, even if things don't go as planned.

* When using affiliate links, be up front with your audience, and don't overdo it. Most readers will be happy to help support your site, but if you use too many links, you'll come across as a sleazy salesman. I have affiliate links for MadMimi (my e-mail list provider) and Moo.com (where I order my business cards). Some bloggers link to their web hosting provider or

Wordpress theme.

* You can use affiliate links on your own site to promote e-books sold on Amazon. However, keep in mind that it's against their Terms of Service to use affiliate links WITHIN Amazon e-books.

Finances & Job Searching

Whether you're a recent college grad just entering the work-force, or you've been laid off after a long career, chances are you're dealing with some degree of debt. While carrying debt is never a good thing, remember that you aren't alone. The average student loan debt for the class of 2014 is over $30,000,[1] and as many as 35% Americans have some amount of unpaid bills in collections.[2]

The first step is to forgive yourself for getting into debt. You couldn't have known that the economy would turn south, or that your college degree wouldn't lead to the job or salary you expected. You won't be able to get out of debt overnight, so find ways to manage your stress levels along the way.

Here are some tools than can help you to keep track of your expenses and reduce the amount you owe to creditors.

Money Management

If you haven't yet signed up for an online budgeting service, that should be your first step. Mint is a free service that keeps track of all of your expenses, and lets you compare spending in various categories over the course of the month.

You can set limits on how much you want to spend on each category — say, food or clothing — and you'll receive alerts whenever you go over-budget. It's a great way to see where your money's going — did you *really* spend that much on movies last month? — and adjust your habits accordingly. Not only that, but you can turn it into a kind of game, trying to keep the numbers improving each month.

There are several other services out that provide budgeting tools. Magnify Money looks at your accounts to find ways you can save by eliminating fees, and earning interest or cashback offers. ReadyForZero creates a personalized debt-payment plan with graphs to help you visualize your progress.

If you're serious about reforming the way you use your money, consider switching over to Simple Bank, an online banking service that provides built-in budgeting via a smartphone app. Simple Bank calculates and categorizes your transactions instantaneously, letting you know how much is "Safe-to-Spend." You can set goals, schedule recurring payments, and estimate upcoming expenses. Withdrawing cash from many ATMs is entirely free.

Finally, stop paying unnecessary PayPal fees every time you transfer money. New services like Dwolla, Venmo, and Square Cash make it cheaper and easier than ever to send money to friends. Just link your bank account or debit card and you're good to go.

Peer-to-Peer Lending

One option to consolidate your credit card debt is to take out a personal loan. In the past, this meant going through a traditional banking service and navigating the associated fees and bureaucracy. Ultimately, the process could be just as frustrating as paying off the credit cards directly.

Lately, peer-to-peer lending services are becoming a popular alternative. While on the surface, they function a lot like a traditional loan, they're funded by a few dozen individual lenders, rather than a bank. This means your interest fees won't be subsidizing Chase Bank or BOA — though you won't, of course, know whether the individuals bankrolling your loan are any more ethical. (Let's assume they are.)

Lending Club and Prosper are two of the most well-known peer-to-peer lending services. You can apply for a loan directly on their website by providing the necessary pay-stubs and/or paperwork, and receive the funds deposited into your bank account. Each month, your payment amount will be deducted from you bank account, saving you the trouble of sending in a paper check.

Be sure to look closely at the transaction fees and interest rates beforehand. Make sure that you'll actually be saving money in the long-term, and that the monthly payments aren't more than you can afford.

Another up-and-coming lending service is Upstart, which bases your loan amount and interest rate on your GPA, educational background, and expected earnings. The idea, as they put it, is that you're "more than your credit score". There's no telling if services like this will truly change the financial industry, but it's great to see a range of alternatives for those of us who prefer not to patronize the big banking sector.

If you're looking for a business loan, a service called Kabbage offers lines of credit to small business owners for six months at a time. This is especially useful for people earning income from Etsy or Ebay. You can link directly to those services in the application process to demonstrate that you have sufficient business income to pay off the loan. Another service, Clovest, helps small businesses raise loans directly from their communities.

Remember that all of these services can be approached from the other side too — as a lender. If you have extra money that you want to invest, peer-to-peer lending can be a great way to make small but stable returns on your assets. A service called Kiva lets you offer "micro-loans" to budding entrepreneurs in developing countries. Because of exchange rates, a small loan from you can make a big difference to a rural community or business venture, at a low risk of default.

Lastly, there's Puddle, which lets you pool resources with friends, family, or business partners. Each of you contributes a small amount to the puddle (say, $200), and you have the freedom to withdraw funds when you need them, so long as you pay them back in a designated time frame.

Job Searching

Whether you're unemployed and looking for work, or a freelancer in need of a full-time income, the job search can be a frustrating process. Either your resume will be over-looked in the shuffle, or else the opportunity will be too good to be true.

One new service, Lynxly, helps recent college grads find jobs at up-and-coming startups. If you've dreamed about working at TaskRabbit or Airbnb, but don't have a technical background, they can help you find a non-technical job at an up-and-coming tech company.

Another site, The Muse, offers career advice and insight into company culture, so you know what qualities businesses are looking for in their employees. Should you act casual or more professional? Do they like self-starters, or instruction-followers?

Likewise, Jobsuitors functions as a kind of job-matching service, taking your skills, personality, and experience into account before connecting you with the appropriate job listings. In today's job market, you need to find ways to stand out from the crowd.

Sites Mentioned

Mint.com
MagnifyMoney.com

ReadyforZero.com
Simple.com
Dwolla.com
Venmo.com
Square.com/cash
LendingClub.com
Prosper.com
Upstart.com
Kabbage.com
Clovest.com
Kiva.org
Puddle.com
Lynxly.com
TheMuse.com
JobSuitors.com

Tips

* As with any of the advice in this book, be advised to proceed at your own risk. While I've used some of the services in this chapter, I can't possible vet and vouch for every financial service out there. Do your own research, and read online reviews before signing up for anything.

* Some sites, like Mint, will require you to provide financial passwords in order to calculate your bank account and credit card balances. Make sure that any

site you use is legitimate and uses secure encryption before turning over financial details.

* Too many budget alerts can get overwhelming. Don't be afraid to turn off some notifications if the constant reminder of your bills or credit card debt is stressing you out. Instead, you can check in on a set schedule — once per day or week — to look over your expenses.

* Simple Bank has been great for my purposes, but one downside is that customers don't have the option of ordering a personalized checkbook. You'll have to request each check individually, which Simple will mail directly to the recipient.

* While peer-to-peer lending may sound nice and friendly, remember that you're still dealing with a financial business. When I applied for a loan with Lending Club, the experience was not entirely different from interacting with a big bank.

* With both Prosper and Lending Club, I received lots of junk mail (both snail and e-mail), encouraging me to check out new loan offers. Be wary of any "pre-approved" offers, and make sure that the rate offered matches the rate you were promised.

* If you're struggle to pay your student loans, see if an

Income-Based Repayment Program is an option; it may be a better fit than simply deferring them.

* When applying for jobs, don't be afraid to follow up by e-mail or Twitter. Even a simple tweet can get a company's attention, so they'll know to look out for your application when they start going through resumes.

* If you don't get the job, be gracious and stay in touch! Chances are you were competing with a large, highly-qualified pool of applicants, so don't take it personally if you get passed over. Stay on good terms with the company and ask them to keep you in the loop for future positions or related gigs.

---

[1] http://blogs.wsj.com/numbers/congatulations-to-class-of-2014-the-most-indebted-ever-1368/
[2] http://www.huffingtonpost.com/2014/07/29/americans-in-debt_n_5629137.html

Entrepreneurship

One trend that has grown hand-in-hand with the Sharing Economy in recent years is the "solo-preneneur" or "micro-entrepreneur" movement. Rather than raising lots of capital or hiring employees up-front, solopreneurs start small, building a business from the ground up.

By leveraging the latest technology, many solopreneurs can run their business on-the-go, or build up a client base in multiple cities. When they do hire employees, they can hire from anywhere in the world, keeping their team functioning smoothly via Skype and other online services.

In this chapter, we'll look at some small business models, as well as the tools these entrepreneurs use to keep their business running. While you may not be ready to build a business of your own, many of the tools in this section can be used for personal productivity too.

Community Forum

One of my favorite business models is the community-based forum, in which members pay a monthly fee for access to resources, video trainings, and other exclusive content. Joining a forum can be an especially great way to connect with business partners and clients when you're just starting out.

At Puttylike, Emilie Wapnick runs a community for "multipotentialites" — people who have many interests and can't just choose one. For $19/month, members have access to the forum, weekly updates, and regularly-scheduled video chats with other community members.

I've been a member of the Puttytribe for almost two years now and made dozens of great connections through the site. I've bartered for services with other members, and even received personalized coaching from a finance blogger in exchange for feedback and a testimonial.

Other popular forums include the Bootstrapper Guild, which helps entrepreneurs launch do-it-yourself business projects, and Fizzle, which offers video trainings and other business resources. Most forums have a discount for your first month so you can check it out and see if it's a good fit for you.

Curious about starting up a community of your own? Ning lets you design and customize your own membership site for $25/month. It's the same platform used to power the Puttytribe and many other online forums. Why not start up a home for other people who share your skills or creative interests?

Subscription Services

Another popular business model is the subscription box service, which functions like a beer- or wine-of-the-month club. I mentioned in Chapter 5 that I spent some time working for Lootcrate, a company that ships "geek and gamer" boxes out to customers each month.

Matt and Chris, the co-founders, started the company in 2012, with very low overhead and upfront costs. They marketed the service in advance, before even buying any inventory. When customers signed up for a subscription, they used that money to purchase the promised items and ship the boxes — first, from their own living room, and later, as the company grew, from a rented office.

Their subscriber base increased each month, as they reached out to bloggers and Youtube stars to spread the word. By the time I left, they had grown from having just a handful of subscribers, to tens of thousands — without ever having to raise money from outside investors.

Not every subscription box service will have the same growth rate, but compared to other kinds of companies, it's a remarkably low-risk business model. Even if it fails, and all of your subscribers cancel, the most you'll be stuck with is a single month's worth of inventory. Plus, rather than hiring lots of employees, you can start off small and scale the company as you go.

Tyler Tervooren (of the Bootstrapper Guild) launched a coffee-subscription company called BrewPony. Other services include Nature Box (healthy snacks), the Dollar Shave Club (razors),

Bugsy's Box (dog toys and treats) and Quarterly, which ships boxes curated by a range of bloggers and celebrities, including Pharrell Williams and Bill Nye. Can you tap into a subscription market that hasn't been reached yet?

Productivity Tools

When juggling multiple business projects, or co-ordinating with long-distance colleagues, how do solo-preneurs and small business owners stay sane? Many of them rely on productivity apps for their computers and smartphones. These kinds of apps sync to "the cloud", backing up your files so that nothing gets lost.

For writing and note-taking, Evernote is my preferred option. It syncs between all of your devices, so a to-do list that you've typed on your iPhone will automatically show up on your laptop when you get home. You can even record audio reminders directly into your notes.

When it comes to sharing audio and video, Dropbox is the way to go. It stores your files in a private folder, so that only people you've shared the link with can access it. It's a great way to send a rough cut of a video project to your client; they can download the finished product directly to their computer.

If you want to backup your entire computer, I recommend Crashplan, an affordable service that continually backs up your files, ensuring that you can access them in an instant if your computer breaks down or is lost or stolen. To keep track of my usernames and log-in information, I use Lastpass, a service that generates hard-to-break passwords and fills them out for me whenever I log into an account.

What about wi-fi security when using the Internet your favorite coffeeshops? Cloak creates a VPN (a virtual private network), ensuring that any information you send over wi-fi (including passwords, e-mails, and financial data) is secure and encrypted. It works both on your laptop AND your smartphone.

Finally, Karma is a device that lets you bring your wi-fi on the go with you — so you can literally work from the beach or on the metro. You can purchase several GB of data up-front, and get 100MB of free data every time someone connects to Karma using your connection.

Accountability Groups

Many entrepreneurs find it useful to start a "mastermind" or "accountability" group.[1] This is a group that meets several times per month, in person or via Skype, to discuss on-going projects, set goals, brainstorm problems, and generally hold each other accountable for getting things done.

There are many ways to structure a mastermind group, but I recommend starting with 3 or 4 members and meeting every other week for 2 hours. This is plenty of time for each person to get a chance to discuss their current goals, without getting too side-tracked by specific details.

If you don't yet have anyone you'd like to start a group with, see if you can find a local group that's open to the public. Many co-working spaces have ongoing meetups and brainstorming sessions at which new members are welcome.

Sites Mentioned

Puttylike.com

BootstrapperGuild.com

Fizzle.co

Ning.com

LootCrate.com

BrewPony.com

NatureBox.com

DollarShaveClub.com

BugsysBox.com

Quarterly.co

Evernote.com

Dropbox.com

Crashplan.com

Lastpass.com

GetCloak.com

YourKarma.com

Tips

* A good community forum is one where members actively contribute and add value for each other. You don't want new members signing up only to find an empty house. Offer free memberships to your most loyal readers to start the process and get people excited about joining the community.

* Most successful forums start off as a blog, and only gradually move the conversation to a message board. If you don't have lots of readers actively commenting on your blog already, then you probably don't have the critical mass needed to start a forum.

* Remember, when starting a business, you don't have to invest in lots of advertising or inventory up front. Start with a "minimum-viable product" — the bare bones of your service — and see if people show any interest. Be prepared to build out from there.

* For a subscription box service, it's OK to let subscribers know that you're just starting out. Be honest with them: "We can only launch if we reach 500 customers by July 1st, so please help us spread the word! If we don't reach our target, our boxes won't ship and we'll refund your money."

* When starting a mastermind group, make sure that

your members share similar goals and are more-or-less at the same stage in their business. If one of your members is making a full-time living selling jewelry on Etsy, while another is casually starting a business in their spare time, chances are they won't have as much useful advice to share with each other — or the conversation will be very one-sided.

* Don't be afraid to set rules for your mastermind group. Some groups find it useful to write down a set of guidelines or repeat a mission statement before each meeting. The whole point of the group is accountability — so if you can't count on your members to be there on time, fully invested in the conversation, they probably aren't a good fit for the group.

---

[1] http://lifehack.org/articles/productivity/how-to-start-and-run-a-mastermind-group.html

Community

It's time to come full circle, and return to some of the ideas that we brought up in the first chapter — specifically, how the Sharing Economy, entrepreneurship, and community-building platforms can help create more vibrant neighborhoods.

We've looked into meal-sharing networks like Feastly, home-sharing sites like Airbnb, car-sharing services, and more. These sites can be a great way to explore new places, and connect with like-minded people when you travel.

But what if you're more interested in connecting with people who live in your neighborhood — locals rather than tourists? What if you like the idea of sharing access to resources, but you feel a little uneasy about monetary transactions?

Here are some ways to build up community in your neighborhood, both online and off.

Neighborhood Networks

NextDoor is a private social network for individual neighborhoods. Think of it as kind of like a closed Facebook group — without the ads! — where the people on your street can announce yard sales, block parties, and more.

Only people in your neighborhood can access the group, and you'll have to verify your address with a postcard to ensure that you actually live where you say you do. Your address won't be shared, of course, but you'll be able to create a profile to let people know a little bit about yourself.

When I signed up for NextDoor in my Portland community, I received several "Welcome to the neighborhood!" messages from people nearby. It's a great way to break the ice and avoid the awkwardness of not knowing anyone in your part of town. Check out ShareTribe, StreetBank, and Peerby for similar services.

Another great tool is Switchboard, a community-based site where you can ask for and offer goods, services, or even advice. Think of it like the bulletin boards you might see at a coffee-shop, covered in flyers for yoga instructors, piano teachers, and after-school plays. While NextDoor is focused on geographical neighborhoods, Switchboard is intended for small groups and organizations, such as a college, church, or small business association.

If you're a bit more ambitious with your community-building, NationBuilder is an all-in-one tool for grass-roots movements and social causes. It's been used to run political campaigns, union events, and off-line protests. Not only will it keep a database of all your supporters, but you'll be able to reach out to them by e-mail or text, sell tickets to events, and launch fundraising campaigns directly through the site.

For one-off events, you can try EventBrite, which lets you sell tickets online for in-person events. It's a great way to promote your band's show or the launch party for your new book. You can set the number of tickets available, arrange for various price levels, and even scan your guests' barcodes at the door with a smartphone app. No more paper tickets and cash registers to worry about!

Finally, Meetup is one of the oldest social networks out there. Twelve years after launching, it's still an active hub for community events of all kinds. You can join a group — say, a hiking club or a writer's critique group — and receive updates whenever a new event is schedule. Browse the local homepage to find events in your city. If you don't see what you're looking for, create a group of your own.

Time Banks & Local Economies

Community exchanges and other kinds of local networks are nothing new; the Internet has just made it easier to get involved. If you're a bit more old-school, and want to take part in the Sharing Economy off-line, consider joining a neighborhood time-bank or skillshare.

Time banks function like an unofficial currency — in most cases, an hour of work that you contribute to the group will earn you an hour of someone else's labor. For example, you could contribute an hour of gardening and receive an hour of housekeeping or cooking in return.

Some time banks provide additional deals to members, such as reduced-fare metro passes. To find a time bank in your area, check out the directory at TimeBanks USA. You can also join a "global" time-bank network at TimeRepublik.

Other communities have taken the idea a step further. Cities like Portland, ME, Ithaca, NY, and Berkshire, MA have created their own local currencies that can be redeemed at stores and businesses just like real cash. It's a great way of encouraging community members to support their local economy.

Each year, near Reno, NV, the Burning Man festival relies on a "gift economy," meaning that no money is exchanged for the duration of the festival. Participants "gift" music, art, and food to each other, creating a temporary community away from corporate sponsorship and consumerism.

In Portland, OR, a small business called FloatHQ offers a robust artist program, in which writers, musicians, and even chefs receive free floatation therapy in return for sharing their creative work. The Oregon Public House is a volunteer-run, non-profit pub that donates proceeds to one of several local charities. Don't rule out the role that barter, trade, and gift-giving can play in your business!

Co-Working Spaces

Another growing trend among community-minded entrepreneurs is the concept of a "co-working" space. Rather than renting out an entire office for your business, co-working spaces allow you to share the environment with other businesses or solopreneurs.

Some co-working spaces are simple and low-key, like a coffee-shop, while others include all sorts of amenities, including kitchen access, showers, and educational programs. Most places allow you to rent your own desk by the week or month, and also have some desks available for walk-ins.

Here in Portland, a few popular options are NedSpace (a more traditional office environment), The Collective Agency (a "cozy workspace"), and The Forge, a co-working space for non-profits and social enterprises.

Lately, some sites have ventured into the on-demand "desk-sharing" model. DesksNearMe and LiquidSpace let you rent out a single desk by the hour or day, while ShareDesk and PivotDesk can help you find a temporary office for your entire team.

Sites Mentioned

NextDoor.com
ShareTribe.com
StreetBank.com
Peerby.com
SwitchBoardHQ.com
NationBuilder.com
EventBrite.com
Meetup.com

TimeBanks.org

TimeRepublik.com

BerkShares.org

IthacaHours.com

BurningMan.com

FloatHQ.com/float-on/programs

OregonPublicHouse.com

NedSpace.com

CollectiveAgency.co

ForgePortland.com

DesksNear.Me

LiquidSpace.com

ShareDesk.net

PivotDesk.com

Tips

* When you sign up for a Meetup group, be sure to adjust your e-mail and notification settings. Otherwise, you'll be notified every time someone creates an event, leaves a comment, or makes any changes to the group. I like to keep e-mails to a minimum and only receive certain updates.

* Some states have specific rules on internships and unpaid labor. Before offering your customers a free service in exchange for their work, make sure that you aren't violating any local labor laws — and make it's a fair bargain for your business and your customers alike.

* Don't get trapped in a traditional business model. Consider a non-hierarchical structure or employee-owned workspace.

* Even non-profits and gift economies need money to keep things running. Don't try so hard to cut money out of the picture that your business can't stay afloat. There are others ways to give back to the community rather than operating your business at a loss.

* A co-working space can be a great way to kick-start some new energy into a project. Take a "working vacation" by renting out a desk in a neighboring town, or share a space with another small business so you can brainstorm new ideas.

* Can't afford to rent a desk at a co-working space? Start your own un-official one by inviting your colleagues to work from the same coffee-shop one day per week, or create a "virtual" co-working space by connecting with your accountability partners over the Internet.

Thanks for reading!

I'm really grateful that you've taken the time to read this book! I hope you've gotten some useful ideas from it. Remember, there's a LOT of information in this book, and I've only scratched the surface. Be sure to bookmark some chapters for reference, or make a list of the sites that you want to check out later.

The only way that I can keep writing books like these is if you help spread the word. Consider lending a copy to a friend, or buying one for a family member for Christmas. If you have Facebook or Twitter, you can share this link to the e-book with your followers: www.bit.ly/savesharesimplify

Also, don't hesitate to reach out with any questions or suggestions for future books! I'm happy to help you get started on your journey into the Sharing Economy. I also offer specific services, like copywriting and videography, if you need more in-depth support.

You can stop by my blog or check out my Amazon store to find some of my other e-books and offerings. You can also follow me on Twitter or listen to my podcast on iTunes. Thanks again for reading!

Contact Info

Website: www.saulofhearts.com
Email: saulofhearts@gmail.com
Twitter: @saulofhearts
Amazon: http://bit.ly/saulofhearts

Other Books

The Lateral Freelancer: How to Make A Living in the Share Economy http://bit.ly/thelateralfreelancer

What Are Your Boundaries? A Burning Man Travelogue http://bit.ly/morecarrotlessstick

The Rational Hippie: Reflections on World, Travel, Sex & Community http://bit.ly/therationalhippie

Made in the USA
Charleston, SC
24 September 2014